P9-BZT-077

Portable Toilet Cleaner

BY ARNOLD RINGSTAD

Published in the United States of America by The Child's World®
1980 Lookout Drive • Mankato, MN 56003-1705
800-599-READ • www.childsworld.com

Acknowledgments
The Child's World®: Mary Berendes, Publishing Director
Red Line Editorial: Editorial direction
The Design Lab: Design
Amnet: Production

Photographs ©: Don Seabrook/AP Images, cover; Nicholas
de Haan/Shutterstock Images, 5; Johnny Habell/Shutterstock
Images, 6; TFoxFoto/Shutterstock Images, 9; Wally Santana/AP
Images, 10; Rob Griffith/AP Images, 13; Library of Congress,
15; Wasu Watcharadachaphong/Shutterstock Images,
17; Arena Creative/Shutterstock Images, 19; Ike Hayden/
Shutterstock Images, 20

ISBN 9781631436895
LCCN 2014945296

Printed in the United States of America
Mankato, MN
November, 2014
PA02238

ABOUT THE AUTHOR

Arnold Ringstad lives in Minnesota, where he writes and edits books for kids. He once had a job cleaning toilets.

TABLE OF CONTENTS

CHAPTER 1

What Does a Portable Toilet Cleaner Do?

Have you ever been to an outdoor **festival**? Have you watched sports outside? You probably saw portable toilets there. They are large plastic boxes with walls and a door. Inside is a toilet. Some also have a sink. Pipes carry waste away in indoor bathrooms. But there are no pipes in these toilets.

Where does the waste go? Portable toilet cleaners empty the toilets with special equipment. They pump the waste into tanks on trucks. Sometimes this is a very gross job. But it is important. Portable toilets let people hold large events outside. They safely keep waste away from crowds. This stops people from getting sick. It is up to workers to make sure toilets stay clean.

Some toilets have
urinals in addition
to seats.

Portable toilets are often found at construction sites.

People always need bathrooms. This means workers are always needed too. People end up with this job for all kinds of reasons. For some, it pays well. Some people enjoy the work.

Some workers like keeping things clean. One worker in Oregon says, "We're in the business to clean things. I don't like my bathroom to be dirty at my house. . . I want my toilets to be clean out on the street."

For others it is a family business. One cleaner in California began working with his dad almost 20 years ago. He later started his own portable toilet company.

DISGUSTING!
Cleaners deal with lots of waste. One company in Oregon owns 27,000 toilets. The company's workers handle up to 1 million gallons (3.8 million L) of human waste in a month! It would take 20,000 bathtubs to hold that much waste!

A Day on the Job

Portable toilet cleaners do more than just clean all day. They spend time answering phones. They order equipment. They keep customers happy. If they did not do these things they would have no toilets to clean and no **gear** to clean with.

Workers plan out the path they will drive. These paths take them to every toilet they must clean. The paths may change often. New customers may be added. An old one may leave. Different paths may be used on different days. They can also change with the seasons. This means that portable toilet cleaners get to visit different places every day.

Some companies drive trucks to each toilet and clean the toilets on location. Other companies work differently. They drive to an outdoor event. Workers pick up the used toilets. They load them onto a large truck. Then, they take them

Workers have to be careful not to knock portable toilets onto their sides when moving them into place.

back to the company. They clean all the toilets in one place. Then the toilets are ready for the next event.

Workers must use the right gear to stay clean and safe. They often wear old clothes. They wear things they don't mind getting dirty. They also wear rubber gloves.

Workers use a special hose to suck up waste.

Other gear includes an apron and boots. Workers may use a face mask. It keeps out smells. All this gear makes the job safer and less gross. Workers also fix toilets if they are broken. They bring along the tools they might need.

Workers drive special trucks. The trucks have large tanks. They also have a pump and a hose. The hose is much larger than a garden hose. It may be several inches wide. The worker parks the truck next to a toilet. Then the worker pulls the hose off the truck. He or she brings the hose into the toilet. The hose goes down into the toilet's base. Then the worker turns on the pump. It sounds like a loud vacuum cleaner. The pump pulls waste through the hose. It fills the truck's tank. After a few minutes, the toilet is empty.

DISGUSTING!
Workers sometimes make mistakes that are gross. A worker in California took off the hose at the wrong time. Waste sprayed out of the hose. The worker and the truck got covered in waste.

Next, the worker cleans the toilet. There are different ways to do this. A worker may use a mop to scrub the walls and floor. Other times, a pressure washer is used. These machines spray water at high speed. Workers must be careful. Waste could spray out of the toilet. Their gear keeps them safe and clean. The last step is to refill the supplies inside. Workers add toilet paper. They may replace the soap if the unit has a sink.

The work changes each season. In many places, summer weather is warm. This means there are more outdoor events. A cleaner may work 40 hours a week in winter. In the summer,

TECHNOLOGY
Trucks carry lots of waste. This means they don't have to stop often to empty their tanks. This saves gas. Large trucks carry 1,000–2,000 gallons (3,800–7,600 L) of waste. Trucks have separate tanks for clean water for the pressure washer.

Portable toilets are useful after natural disasters like earthquakes when indoor plumbing isn't working.

this could go up to 55 hours. Workers clean between 10 and 60 toilets each day.

Emptying toilets in cold weather can be tougher. The waste may freeze in the bottom of the toilet. Workers can put salt inside so the waste melts. Once the waste has melted, cleaners can use the hose to remove it.

CHAPTER 3

The History of Portable Toilets

Portable toilets have been around for more than 60 years. They were first used at shipyards. These are places where people build ships. At one shipyard in California, bosses noticed time was being wasted. Every time a worker had to go to the bathroom, he had to walk a long way. Companies built bathrooms on the ships to save time. The bathrooms were taken down after the ships were built.

Later, the toilets were used in more places. They were useful at outdoor events. They were also used at construction sites. In the 1950s, companies started building them out of metal. In the 1980s, they started using plastic. Plastic is still used today.

The government used portable toilets at camps they set up during the Great Depression.

The most toilets ever used at one event was 5,000. The event was when Barack Obama became president in 2009. This happened in Washington, DC.

Some people think all portable toilets are gross. They think of thin plastic walls. They remember bad smells. But not all are like this. Some look like regular bathrooms. They come on large trailers. They are much larger than most portable toilets.

The nicest toilets are found at fancy events. This includes outdoor weddings. They may also be found on movie sets. In these places, people pay extra for a nicer restroom.

These toilets have many special features. The toilets flush. This makes it smell better than

TECHNOLOGY

Portable toilets have come a long way. Now they are much nicer than the first wooden ones. Some of the best have music players and wooden floors. If an event is in a hot place, the restroom may even have air conditioning!

Some portable toilets are built into the back of large trucks.

if chemicals were used. Toilets are made of **porcelain** rather than plastic. Some bathrooms have more than one toilet. They have sinks with mirrors. Rugs, paintings, and flowers decorate the inside.

CHAPTER 4

Overcoming Problems

The biggest problem with portable toilets is the smell. There's no way to get around it—human waste smells bad. But there are ways to make toilets better. New kinds of **chemicals** can be used in the toilet. They make it smell better. Workers sometimes spray air freshener when they clean a toilet.

Sometimes portable toilets get knocked over. This can be very gross. Strong winds can push a toilet onto its side. People can also push a toilet over. Waste spills out from the base. It flows onto the walls and door. A toilet normally takes five minutes to clean. One that's been knocked over can take 15 minutes.

There are easy ways to prevent this. Toilets can be heavier or have wider bases. This makes it harder for them to fall over. Toilets can also be tied down to the ground. Doing this can prevent a big mess later.

Portable toilets smell bad, but sometimes they are the only option.

CALUMET CITY PUBLIC LIBRARY

19

Portable toilets should be placed far away from storm drains.

Workers must be careful when pumping waste. Waste can spill from the toilet, hose, or truck. If it flows into a **storm drain** it could **contaminate** the water. Waste carries germs that cause disease. The chemicals that were put in the toilet also spill out.

Workers can help prevent this. A hole in a toilet or a rip in a hose can cause a spill. Workers fix toilets, hoses, and trucks when they are broken. Companies also place toilets far from storm drains. They quickly report any spills that happen.

Cleaning portable toilets can be a gross job. But portable toilet cleaners make the world safer and less gross for everyone else.

TECHNOLOGY

New cleaning systems make workers' jobs less gross. One system looks a little like a lawn sprinkler. The worker attaches it to a water hose. Then he or she puts it in the toilet. The worker closes the door. The system spins around and sprays water. After a few minutes the worker opens the door. After it dries, the toilet is clean and ready for use.

GLOSSARY

chemicals (KEM-i-kulz) Chemicals are materials or liquids that are prepared for a certain use. Workers use chemicals to break down waste in portable toilets.

contaminate (kun-TAM-uh-nate) To contaminate something is to make it dirty. Waste can contaminate water.

festival (FES-tuh-vul) A festival is a party, often held outdoors. A festival usually needs many portable toilets.

gear (geer) Gear is clothing or equipment used for a certain purpose. Portable toilet cleaners use gear to keep them clean and safe.

porcelain (POR-suh-lin) Porcelain is a hard, white material. Toilets in normal restrooms are sometimes made of porcelain.

storm drain (storm drayn) A storm drain is a hole in a paved area that carries rainwater away, usually into a body of water. A portable toilet should be kept away from a storm drain in case of a spill.

TO LEARN MORE

BOOKS

Boyer, Crispin. *That's Gross!: Icky Facts That Will Test Your Gross-Out Factor*. Washington, DC: National Geographic, 2012.

Macaulay, David. *Toilet: How It Works*. New York: Roaring Brook Press, 2013.

WEB SITES

Visit our Web site for links about portable toilet cleaners: *childsworld.com/links*

Note to Parents, Teachers, and Librarians: We routinely verify our Web links to make sure they are safe and active sites. So encourage your readers to check them out!

INDEX